KENNEDY
Through the Lens

How Photography and Television Revealed and Shaped an Extraordinary Leader

Martin W. Sandler

WALKER & COMPANY
New York

INTRODUCTION

His name was John Fitzgerald Kennedy and he was the youngest person ever elected president of the United States. He won the country's highest office by the narrowest of margins and led the country for little more than a thousand days. Yet in that short time, he steered the nation and the world through a nuclear crisis that threatened the planet's very existence, brought hope to millions of Americans who for so long had been denied equality and opportunity, and launched the United States on its journey to the moon and the stars.

He was handsome, witty, and possessed with a genius for words not present in the presidency since Abraham Lincoln graced the White House. His eloquent calls for peace ("Mankind must put an end to war—or war will put an end to mankind"), justice ("One true measure of a nation is its success in fulfilling the promise of a better life for each of its members"), and national service ("For of those to whom much is given, much is required") inspired millions of his fellow citizens—particularly young people—more profoundly than any president who had come before him.

At a time when photography had become more accessible and more popular than ever, an era in which the world was introduced to the miracle of television, John F. Kennedy became our most photogenic president. Through tens of thousands of photographs and the television screen, the nation became enchanted with his charisma, his beautiful and charming wife, and their equally photogenic children. And at a time of unprecedented world crises, photography and television would best reveal and most profoundly shape the life and career of a president who is still so fondly remembered.

AN IMMORTAL ADDRESS

"In the long history of the world, only a few generations have been granted the role of defending freedom in its hour of maximum danger. I do not shrink from this responsibility—I welcome it."

On January 20, 1961, John Fitzgerald Kennedy, the first American president born in the twentieth century, stood on the steps of the United States Capitol and delivered one of the most memorable inaugural addresses in the nation's history. Aware that he was assuming office at a dangerous time—when the most powerful weapons the world had ever known threatened the very survival of the human race—the young president proclaimed that he was more than ready to meet this and the other substantial challenges that faced him. "Let the word go forth from this time and place, to friend and foe alike," he declared, "that the torch has been passed to a new generation of Americans—born in this century, tempered by war, disciplined by a hard and bitter peace, proud of our ancient heritage."

Kennedy called upon the American people to enlist in "a struggle against the common enemies of man: tyranny, poverty, disease, and war itself." Then, in one of the most well-remembered lines ever uttered by any American president, he reminded his fellow citizens of the sacrifices that would need to be made: "Ask not what your country can do for you—ask what you can do for your country."

The man who would affectionately become known as JFK then briefly outlined what he intended to achieve during his time in office. He concluded by acknowledging, "All this will not be finished in the first one hundred days. Nor will it be finished in the first one thousand days, nor in the life of this administration, nor even perhaps in our lifetime on this planet. But let us begin."

ABOVE: John Kennedy shakes hands with his predecessor, Dwight D. Eisenhower. At the time, the seventy-year-old Eisenhower was the oldest president to leave office.

OPPOSITE: John Kennedy wrote and rewrote his inaugural address several times. The result was a speech that was, in the words of historian Tim Hill, "a masterpiece of rhetoric and delivery."

EMBRACING PHOTOGRAPHY

"Change is the law of life. And those who look only to the past or the present are certain to miss the future."

By the time Kennedy entered the White House, new approaches to photography, particularly photojournalism featured in magazines such as *Life, Look, Time,* and *Newsweek,* had become immensely popular. Due to these publications, people had become accustomed to getting their news about people, places, and events from photographs as well as words. This had been made possible by technological developments. The earlier large, bulky, slow cameras had limited the types of pictures photographers could take. By the 1950s, however, photographers were equipped with smaller and lighter cameras that allowed them to capture scenes, and even sequences of scenes, far more rapidly than had once been imagined.

Before Kennedy, American presidents had been wary of the intimacy these new cameras could convey. For the most part, presidents had limited photographers to taking portraits and capturing formal scenes such as the greeting of foreign dignitaries, giving speeches, and signing documents. The day-to-day running of their presidencies and private moments with their families were mostly off-limits.

John Kennedy was the first president to realize how important photographs could be to showing the way he met the challenges of his office. Rather than being wary of what photography might reveal, he regarded it as an ally, not only when it disclosed his working style but also when it revealed his beautiful and talented wife and their charming children. The result was the most complete and intimate visual portrayal of a presidency ever compiled, one that contributed immeasurably to John Kennedy's popularity and effectiveness.

ABOVE: John Kennedy was willing to use personal moments with his family to craft his image as a devoted young father, which helped him to win over the American public. Here, his son, then known as John-John, plays beneath the desk in the Oval Office.

OPPOSITE: Already a celebrity before becoming president, Kennedy became one of the most photographed people in the world.

REMARKABLE PARENTS

"For of those to whom much is given, much is required."

John Kennedy was born into an extraordinary family, which was destined to become one of the best known in all of America. His ancestors had emigrated from Ireland and settled in Boston at a time of great prejudice against Irish Catholics in that city. But John's father, Joseph, was determined to succeed.

After working his way through Harvard University, Joseph Kennedy went into banking, and at the age of twenty-five he became the youngest bank president in America. But he was not satisfied. Stating that his goal was to become a millionaire by thirty-five, he actually became a multimillionaire by establishing a number of thriving businesses ranging from investment and finance firms to one of the first motion-picture companies. By 1934, Joseph's accomplishments had captured the attention of President Franklin D. Roosevelt, who appointed him head of the nation's new Securities and Exchange Commission. Four years later, Roosevelt appointed him United States ambassador to Great Britain.

As ambitious and driven as he was for himself, Joseph Kennedy was even more so as far as his nine children, particularly his boys, were concerned. "My husband is quite a strict father," John's mother, Rose, would state. "He likes the boys to win at sports and everything they try." Joseph Kennedy stated it simply. "Come in a winner," he repeatedly told his four sons. "Second place is no good."

The Kennedys would become a truly remarkable family, due as much to John's mother as to his father. Rose Kennedy was the daughter of one of the most colorful and popular mayors Boston had ever had. She was a devoted parent, stating, "Children should be stimulated by their parents to see, touch, know, understand and appreciate." And at a time when far fewer women were involved in politics than they are today, Rose would continually play an active role in helping her son John rise to the highest office in the land.

ABOVE: Both of John Kennedy's parents appear in this 1907 photograph of a beach party. Rose Fitzgerald (John's mother) is third from the left. Joseph Kennedy Sr. (John's father) is second from the right.

OPPOSITE: This 1938 photograph of the Kennedy family includes future congressmen, senators, war heroes, wives of government officials, and a president of the United States; John is on the far right.

THE FIRST TELEVISION PRESIDENT

"I am certain that … we … will be remembered not for victories or defeats in battle or in politics, but for our contribution to the human spirit."

No invention has ever been embraced so completely and in such great numbers as the television. In the years following TV's introduction to the American public in 1939, barely anyone could afford a television set. Today, the average American home has more TVs than people. Even more important than the numbers, however, is the way that television has affected almost every aspect of our lives, including how we get our news, the way we are entertained, and the way we elect our public officials.

Almost from the beginning, it became clear that television is most effective when it leaves the studio and gives us a front-row seat to the major events of our day. Through television, we have witnessed such historic moments as man's first steps on the moon and the election of the nation's first African American president.

Television has brought such near disasters as the Apollo 13 space mission and such real disasters as the space shuttle *Challenger* explosion directly to our living rooms. And through the television screen we have been eyewitnesses to such horrors as the 9/11 terrorist attacks and seen firsthand the traumas of war.

John Kennedy and television seemed to have been made for each other. He welcomed the constant scrutiny of the TV camera's eye and took expert advantage of the unprecedented exposure it gave him. All the major events of his presidency—his press conferences, his addresses to the American public, his struggles against the forces of communism, his appeals to the nation's youth—were shaped by his understanding of television's unique power to both sway and mold public opinion. For good reason he has been called "America's first television president."

ABOVE: Thanks to the new medium, more people than ever before were able to see an American chief executive at the same time.

OPPOSITE: Commenting on the way John Kennedy used television to his advantage, journalist Hugh Sidey wrote, "He invaded the living rooms of America … and so, in a way, we all claimed him." Here, Kennedy sits for a televised interview with TV newsman Walter Cronkite.

BEGINNINGS

"What really counts is not the immediate act of courage or of valor, but those who bear the struggle day in and day out."

John Kennedy was born on May 29, 1917, the second of nine Kennedy children. Keeping track of so large a family was a great challenge, so Rose Kennedy resorted to preparing file cards on which she recorded such information as each child's medical and dental treatments and the illnesses they suffered.

Unfortunately for young John, also known as Jack, the largest number of cards would be devoted to his illnesses, including chicken pox, whooping cough, and measles. These, however, paled in comparison to his life-threatening bout with scarlet fever when he was two years old. But he developed a quick sense of humor despite his fragile health. By the time he was a teenager, he would tell a friend that if anyone ever wrote a book about him, it would probably devote most of its pages to his medical history.

Other major events in John's childhood often centered around his relationship with his older brother, Joe Jr. This relationship was based on a fierce rivalry—which sometimes came to blows—as well as grudging admiration for each other. John wrote, "I think that if the Kennedy children . . . ever amount to anything, it will be due more to Joe's behavior and his constant example than to any other factor."

Given his father's many ventures, the family moved several times during John's youth, and he attended several different schools. His academic record was never outstanding, but both teachers and fellow students often commented on his charm and wit. When he graduated from high school, his classmates voted him Most Likely to Succeed. No one could have imagined how accurate a prophecy it was.

ABOVE: Even as a youngster, John Kennedy (far left) possessed a winning smile, a quality that would serve him well throughout his life.

OPPOSITE: John grew up in the company of exceptional siblings. Left to right, youngest to oldest, they are: Jean, Robert, Patricia, Eunice, Kathleen, Rosemary, John, and Joe Jr. The final Kennedy, Edward, isn't shown because he hadn't been born yet.

PRELUDE TO GREATNESS

"We celebrate the past to awaken the future."

John Kennedy's grades were never as good as his teachers thought he could attain. He always lagged behind Joe Jr. in the classroom and on the playing field. But, both as a child and as a young adult, he developed qualities that were essential in molding the character of someone destined to reach his country's highest office.

Kennedy loved to read, and he pored over books with a passion rare in someone so young. Among his favorites were books that inspired him to think about people, places, and events much different from those in his own world. Most of all, he loved to read about history, an interest that would prove essential in preparing him for what lay ahead. "History made Jack what he was," his wife would later say. "This little boy, sick so much of the time, reading in bed, reading history."

Early on, he displayed other characteristics that would stay with him all his life and would serve him well. High among them was a fierce sense of loyalty that he showed to all his siblings, particularly his sister Rosemary. Rosemary was intellectually disabled, and from a young age John helped look after her.

Perhaps most important of all, young John Kennedy developed an ability to express himself that would come to characterize him. He was barely in long pants when his grandfather brought him along as he campaigned for governor of Massachusetts. On one stop, his grandfather lifted John up onto a table and announced, "Here's my grandson, the finest grandson in the world!" To the delight of the crowd, the tiny grandson shouted back, "My grandpa is the finest grandpa in the world!" Six-year-old John Kennedy had given his first political speech.

CANTERBURY SCHOOL
NEW MILFORD, CONNECTICUT

Record of John Kennedy, Form II

From November 1 to December 6, 1930.

Any average from 90% to 100% is accounted "Very Good"; from 80% to 90% "Good"; from 70% to 80% "Fair"; from 60% to 70% "Poor"; and below 60% "Unsatisfactory".

SUBJECT	DAILY WORK	EFFORT AND APPLICATION	FORM AVERAGE
English II	86	Good	71.69
Latin II	55	Poor	64.35
History II	77	Good	67.00
Mathematics II	95	Good	61.69
Science II	72	Good	66.62
Religion II	75	Fair	78.46
AVERAGE: 77.00			

This report is not quite so good as the last one. The damage was done chiefly by "Poor" effort in Latin, in which Jack got a mark of 55. He can do better than this. In fact, his average should be well in the 80's.

N.H.

ABOVE: John Kennedy's academic record as a child was far from spectacular. As this report card indicates, he did not always give every subject his full effort.

OPPOSITE: Joe Jr. and John pose with three of their sisters. Although he would not admit it at the time, young John had great admiration for his older brother's abilities.

TURNING POINT

In late 1937, John Kennedy's father was the United States ambassador to Great Britain. With several European countries at odds with each other and gearing themselves for war, it became a pivotal time in the life of John Kennedy as well.

While a student at Harvard, John Kennedy was not certain which career path he wanted to take when two trips to Europe influenced his thinking. The first, a pleasure trip in the summer of 1937, introduced him to the intrigues of world politics. The second, in 1939, convinced him that it was politics he wished to pursue.

By the time Kennedy returned to Harvard for his senior year, Germany had invaded Poland and World War II had begun. Needing a subject for his senior thesis, Kennedy decided to write about a topic he had investigated firsthand during his two European trips: England's lack of preparation for a war that many felt was certain to take place. Never had he worked so hard on a project. But when he finished, he felt he had written something special.

He was not alone. When his father read what

JOHN FITZGERALD KENNEDY
Born May 29, 1917, in Brookline, Massachusetts. Prepared at The Choate School. Home Address: 294 Pondfield Road, Bronxville, New York. Winthrop House. *Crimson* (2–4); Chairman Smoker Committee (1); St. Paul's Catholic Club (1–4). Football (1), Junior Varsity (2); Swimming (1), Squad (2). Golf (1). House Hockey (3, 4); House Swimming (2); House Softball (4). Hasty Pudding-Institute of 1770; Spee Club. Permanent Class Committee. Field of Concentration: Government. Intended Vocation: Law.

his son had written, he was so impressed that he used his contacts to get the work published. Titled *Why England Slept*, the book, which became a bestseller, included a foreword in one of its reprints that would prove remarkably prophetic. Written by *Time* magazine editor Henry R. Luce, it stated, "If John Kennedy is characteristic of the younger generation—and I believe he is—many of us would be happy to have the destinies of this Republic handed over to his generation at once."

ABOVE: John Kennedy's Harvard yearbook entry revealed that, while his field of concentration at college was government, he intended to go into law.

OPPOSITE: John's trips to Europe in 1937 and 1939 broadened his horizons. Here, he poses with a Belgian woman.

WAR HERO

"Any man who may be asked in this century what he did to make his life worthwhile...
can respond... 'I served in the United States Navy.'"

In 1941, alarmed by the way Nazi Germany was overwhelming Europe and by the prospect of Japan joining forces with Germany, both John and Joseph Kennedy Jr. entered military service—John in the navy, Joe Jr. in the naval reserve as a combat pilot.

After the Japanese attacked Pearl Harbor on December 7, 1941, the United States entered World War II. In 1943, John was assigned to the South Pacific, where he was placed in command of a patrol torpedo boat named *PT-109*. On the night of August 1–2, 1943, Kennedy's vessel was suddenly struck and split in half by a Japanese destroyer. Half of Kennedy's crew were killed. Noticing that one of the survivors, Patrick McMahon, had suffered severe burns and was drowning, Kennedy swam over to McMahon and guided him to a large piece of debris that other members of the crew were clinging to.

When the sun came up the next day, Kennedy led his crewmen to a small island several miles away. He managed to get McMahon to the island by clenching the strap from McMahon's life jacket in his teeth and towing him along. Six days later, Kennedy and his men were found by a small group of friendly islanders. Kennedy gave them a coconut shell upon which he had carved a message; the islanders then went off seeking more help. A short time later they returned with aid, and Kennedy and the surviving crew of the *PT-109* were saved.

John returned home a hero and was awarded the U.S. Navy and Marine Corps Medal for his courage and leadership. As far as he was concerned, he had simply done what he needed to do. Later, when asked how he had become a hero, he replied simply, "It was involuntary. They sank my boat."

Above: John Kennedy saved the coconut on which he'd carved, "NAURO ISL ... COMMANDER ... NATIVE KNOWS POS'IT ... HE CAN PILOT ... 11 ALIVE ... NEED SMALL BOAT ... KENNEDY." This led to the rescue of the crew of *PT-109*. When he became president, he proudly displayed it on his desk in the Oval Office.

Opposite: The crew of *PT-109* pose with their commander, Lieutenant John Kennedy (far right). When he was sworn in as president, several of the crew members took part in Kennedy's inaugural festivities.

ENTERING POLITICS

"Today we need a nation of . . . citizens . . . who regard the preservation of freedom as a basic purpose of their daily life."

Although John Kennedy downplayed his heroism following the sinking of *PT-109*, the crew's rescue came at a great personal price. He had injured his back, seriously aggravating a condition that had first appeared in his adolescence, and in June 1944 he was forced to undergo surgery. While he was recuperating, he received the terrible news that Joe Jr. had been killed in the skies over England while attempting to carry out a dangerous bombing mission.

From the time Joe Jr. had been a child, his father had wanted him to become president of the United States. Now, with Joe Jr. gone, this dream was transferred to John. It was an awesome responsibility to have thrust upon him, but thanks to his experiences in Europe and wartime leadership in the Pacific, Kennedy had already begun leaning toward entering politics. In 1946 he announced his candidacy for the United States Congress.

Veteran politicians in the district in which Kennedy was running were convinced that he had little chance for success. How could a millionaire's son win in a district made up mostly of working-class, modest-income families? Ignoring the experts, Kennedy threw himself into the election with a vigor that surprised even his father. Not only did he campaign day and night, but he did so with wit and a sense of humor. For example, during one huge gathering, each of his several opponents was introduced as "a man who came up the hard way." When Kennedy was introduced, there was silence until, with a wide grin, he stated, "I'm the one who didn't come up the hard way." When the election was over and the votes were counted, the man "who didn't come up the hard way" won by a better than two-to-one margin over his closest rival. Twenty-nine-year-old John Kennedy was on his way to Washington DC.

ABOVE: During his early campaigns, John Kennedy was helped immeasurably by his mother and his sisters, who hosted thousands of "tea parties" for potential voters. Here, Rose Kennedy speaks at one of these parties as the candidate looks on.

OPPOSITE: Eunice Kennedy proudly displays her specially made skirt as congressional candidate John Kennedy makes one of his earliest television appearances.

PROFILE IN COURAGE

"Without belittling the courage with which men have died, we should not forget those acts of courage with which men...have lived.*"*

John Kennedy served for six years as a member of the U.S. House of Representatives, twice being reelected by huge margins. But after six years in the House, he became eager to make his mark in an even bigger political arena. In 1952, aided once again by the nonstop efforts of his entire family, he was elected to the U.S. Senate.

Thanks to his charisma and intelligence, Kennedy quickly became one of the Senate's most popular members. He also fell in love, and in 1953 he married Jacqueline Bouvier. But the following year he experienced a serious physical setback when the back injury he had suffered during his *PT-109* heroics flared up. The back pain became so severe that he could no longer avoid or postpone another surgery.

During the many painful months of recuperation, Kennedy decided this was the perfect time to undertake a project that had long been in his mind. Of all human traits, the one he admired most was courage. During the war, Kennedy had dramatically shown that he possessed it. And now he displayed a different type of courage: ignoring the constant pain while researching and writing a book that highlighted certain United States senators throughout history who had risked their careers to fight for things in which they believed. Kennedy called the inspirational book *Profiles in Courage*, and it would become a bestseller and win the Pulitzer Prize—one of literature's highest awards.

By 1956, not only had he been able to resume his Senate duties, but at the Democratic Convention he had come extremely close to being named the party's candidate for vice president. The nationwide television exposure he received convinced millions of Americans that he deserved presidential, not vice presidential, consideration. Four years later, John F. Kennedy stood before a wildly cheering crowd at the Democratic Convention in Los Angeles as his party's nominee for president of the United States.

ABOVE: In *Profiles in Courage*, John Kennedy expressed one of his most important personal beliefs when he wrote, "A man does what he must—in spite of personal consequences, in spite of obstacles and dangers and pressures."

OPPOSITE: Kennedy's serious back operation in 1954 required a long hospital stay. Here, his wife, Jacqueline, a police officer, and a nurse look on as the senator is placed in an ambulance for his return home.

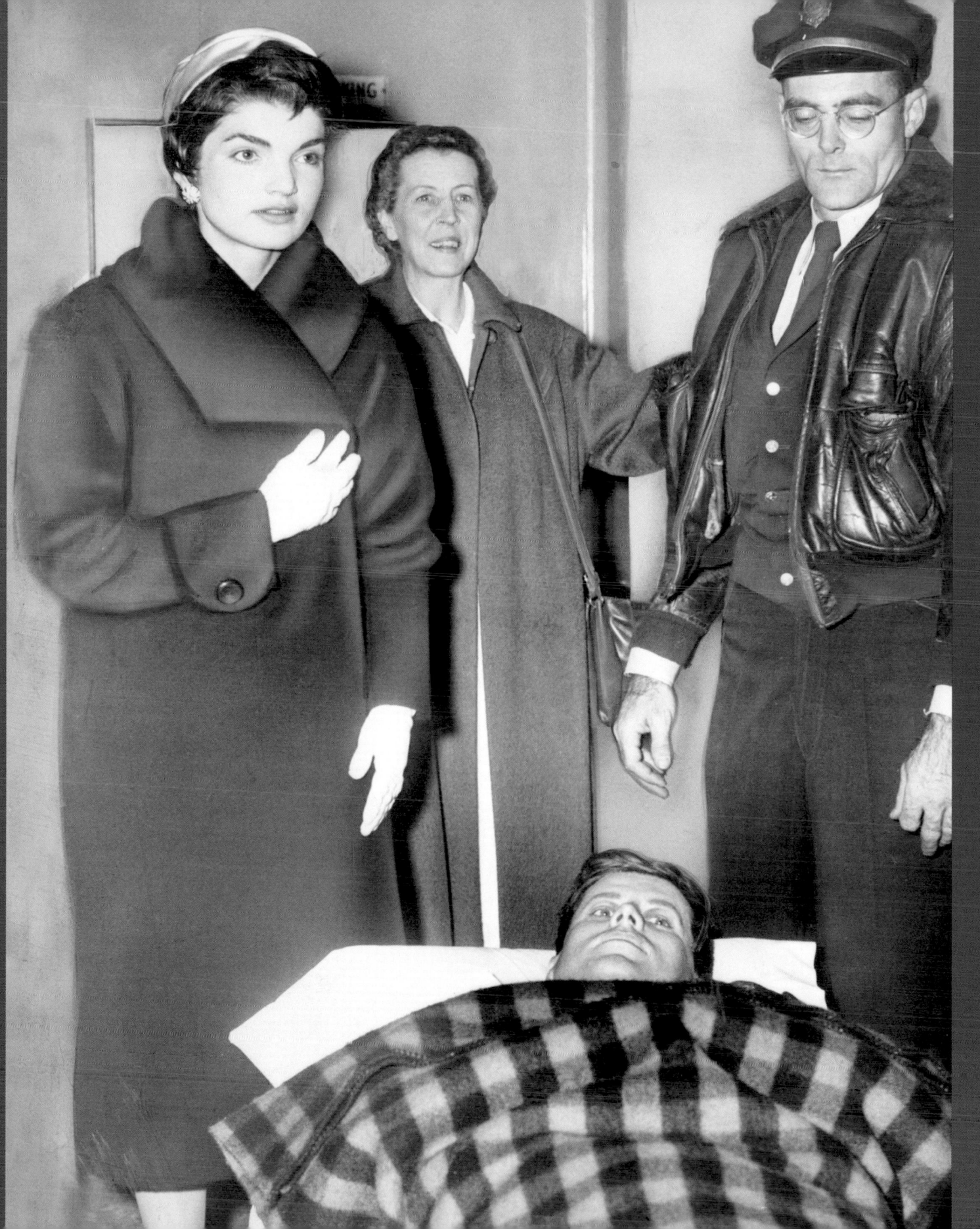

A PRESIDENCY IN COLOR

"We must never forget that art is not a form of propaganda; it is a form of truth."

Before John Kennedy entered the White House, most of the pictures of American presidents were taken in black and white. By the time Kennedy was elected, however, advancements in high-quality color film and in printing paper had reached a point where, for the first time, color photographs became a popular and affordable reality.

The Kennedy presidency was the first to be photographed largely in color. And color photography had a major impact on people's impressions of the president, the First Lady, and their children. Far more than black-and-white images, color photographs were perfect for capturing the glamour that came to be associated with the Kennedy years. Through color photographs, millions of women who avidly followed Jacqueline Kennedy's fashions were best able to get a true look at her latest gowns and dresses. Color photography best captured the splendor of the gala events the Kennedys hosted at the White House. And color photography most effectively conveyed to the public John Kennedy's passion for the sea—particularly sailing the waters off Cape Cod.

Despite these advantages, many photographers in Kennedy's time preferred to continue working in black and white. Some of today's talented photographers share that preference. Still, it is hard to imagine that a picture such as the one on the opposite page would have been as effective in black and white as it is in color.

ABOVE: John Kennedy's love of sailing was a favorite subject of photographers working in color.

OPPOSITE: The advancements that made it possible to photographically capture the splendor of the lights and ornaments on the White House Christmas tree were made not long before John Kennedy became president.

TELEVISION CHANGES POLITICS

"We must think and act not only for the moment but for our time."

Debates have been an integral part of American politics for more than 150 years. However, the debates that took place during the election of 1960 were significantly different from any that had come before. Carried live on the young medium of television by all three national networks, the first debate alone was seen by some seventy million people.

John Kennedy's opponent, Richard Nixon, had been vice president for two terms and was well known throughout the nation. Kennedy, on the other hand, was a newcomer, and polls indicated that many thought him too inexperienced to serve as president. For Kennedy, the television debates presented the opportunity to look presidential in front of the largest audience in American political history.

Most historians agree that the result of the first—and most influential—of the four televised debates was actually determined a little more than a month before it took place. During a campaign stop, Nixon injured

his knee while getting into a car. The knee became so infected that the vice president was hospitalized for two weeks, becoming pale and weak looking from his ordeal.

Nixon's appearance at the all-important first debate was made even worse when aides applied too much white makeup to his face, making him look physically unfit. Kennedy, by contrast, looked young and ready to take on any challenge. Through both his appearance and the informed answers he gave to the debate moderator's questions, Kennedy looked positively presidential.

Studies would later show that of the four million people who made up their minds based on the television debate, three million had voted for Kennedy. American politics would never be the same. From the 1960 election on, how a candidate looked and performed on television would be a major factor in determining who would be the next president of the United States.

ABOVE: Just as John Kennedy acknowledged that the television debates were instrumental in his being elected president, Abraham Lincoln publicly stated that this photograph, in which he appeared "presidential" for the first time, was a vital factor in his election.

OPPOSITE: Throughout the first televised debate, a perspiring Richard Nixon continually wiped his face, an action that did not play well with the voters.

ROAD TO THE WHITE HOUSE

"The New Frontier of which I speak is not a set of promises—it is a set of challenges. It sums up not what I intend to offer the American people, but what I intend to ask of them."

He was one of the youngest men ever nominated for the presidency. And it soon became clear that he was one of the most articulate, inspirational speakers the nation had ever encountered. As he delivered his speech accepting his nomination to a crowd thrilled with the youth, vigor, and enthusiasm of its candidate, Kennedy stated, "We stand today on the edge of a New Frontier.... Beyond that frontier are the uncharted areas of science and space, unsolved problems of peace and war, unconquered pockets of ignorance and prejudice, unanswered questions of poverty and surplus." Then he hit the campaign trail, vowing to take on all these challenges.

Ignoring the back that never stopped aching, and determined to reach out to as many voters as possible, he traveled more than seventy-five thousand miles in his campaign plane, the *Caroline*, giving speech after speech. Everywhere Kennedy spoke he drew enormous crowds. Increasingly it appeared that the nation was responding to his message that it was time for a new, more energetic leadership.

The experts knew the election was going to be close. No one, however, predicted that it would be the closest in the nation's history. On November 8, almost seventy million Americans went to the polls. When all the ballots were finally counted at 5:45 a.m. the next day, Kennedy had received 49.7 percent of the vote, just 0.2 percent more than opponent Vice President Richard Nixon's 49.5 percent. At the age of forty-three, John Fitzgerald Kennedy was about to become president of the United States.

ABOVE: During his campaign for the presidency, John Kennedy tried to personally reach as many voters as he could. Here, he takes a coffee break with supporters in Nashua, New Hampshire.

OPPOSITE: Kennedy's articulate and dynamic speaking style helped him win over many voters.

BATTLING PREJUDICE

"I am not the Catholic candidate for president. I am the Democratic candidate for president who happens to be a Catholic."

Television's new and powerful influence was not the only important mark of the 1960 presidential campaign. John Kennedy, who happened to be Catholic, also confronted an issue that would have an enormous impact on the future of presidential politics: religion. In Kennedy's case, anti-Catholic prejudice threatened to derail his bid for the presidency. A large number of people believed that, if he was elected, many of his decisions would be guided by the head of the Catholic Church, the pope.

Kennedy had actually been forced to deal with the problem even before he won his party's nomination. Speaking to a large crowd during West Virginia's primary election, he stated, "Nobody asked me if I was Catholic when I joined the U.S. Navy. Nobody asked my brother if he was a Catholic or Protestant before he climbed into an American bomber plane to fly his last mission."

Kennedy's speech won over the West Virginia crowd, but once he began campaigning for the presidency, the issue became even more intense. Realizing he had to meet the situation head-on, he arranged to address a large audience of non-Catholic ministers. Speaking directly to those in the auditorium and to a large television audience, Kennedy declared, "I believe in an America . . . where no public official either requests or accepts instructions on public policy from the pope . . . or any other [religious] source." Kennedy finished his speech to prolonged applause. A poll of television viewers revealed that his remarks had met with overwhelming approval.

It was a significant victory for the candidate, but it was even more important for the future of the nation. Today we live in a country where a woman, Hillary Clinton, has been a serious candidate for the presidency and an African American, Barack Obama, has been elected to the highest office in the land. It was John F. Kennedy who helped pave the way.

ABOVE: The 2007–08 race for the Democratic Party's presidential nomination was characterized by the spirited contest between Barack Obama and Hillary Clinton. After his election, Obama selected Clinton to be his secretary of state.

OPPOSITE: A young John Kennedy (back row, second from left) poses with his parents and his brothers and sisters in the Vatican before receiving an audience with the pope.

A UNIQUE FIRST LADY

John Kennedy did not enter the White House alone. By his side was his charismatic and talented wife. Like her husband, Jacqueline Kennedy had enjoyed a privileged upbringing, which included private schools, study abroad in Paris, and a degree in art. An accomplished horsewoman since childhood, she had won several national riding championships. But she was also determined to do more with her life than engage in shopping sprees and attend fancy dinners. She met Senator Kennedy at a time when relatively few women held full-time professional jobs. Yet she was a photographer and a reporter for the *Washington Times-Herald* newspaper.

Both her job and Kennedy's kept them constantly on the go, but somehow they completed a successful courtship, much of it by long-distance telephone. Not surprisingly, given the prominence of their families, their wedding was a society event—complete with eight hundred guests, a blessing sent by the pope, and extraordinary media coverage. It was only the beginning. For just as the handsome and dynamic John Kennedy would bring a youthful spirit to the presidency, so too would Jacqueline bring irresistible charm to the White House. The media could not resist either one.

She was only thirty-one when she became First Lady. She was beautiful, elegant, and intelligent—and the nation fell in love with her. Almost immediately she became a trendsetter. Women everywhere copied her hairstyles, the design of her clothes, even the type of hats she wore.

But Jacqueline Kennedy was interested in much more than fashion. Endowed with a deep respect for history and a love of music, literature, and all the arts, she and her husband would bring a whole new dimension to both the White House and the presidency.

ABOVE: During her husband's presidency, Jacqueline Kennedy traveled the world on behalf of the United States. Here, she receives a corsage from a youngster upon her arrival in Caracas, Venezuela.

OPPOSITE: Everywhere she went, all eyes were on Jacqueline. Here, she and the president play host to France's minister for cultural affairs.

A TELEVISED TOUR OF THE WHITE HOUSE

"Mrs. Kennedy is organizing herself. It takes longer, but, of course, she looks better than we do when she does it."

When Jacqueline Kennedy was a child, her mother took her and her sister on a tour of the White House. Young as she was, Jackie was shocked to see how few historical furnishings were in evidence. Even before her husband's inauguration, Mrs. Kennedy began making plans for a complete restoration of the White House's historic rooms. Under her direction, and with the aid of the nation's first-ever White House curator, whose appointment she had arranged, all of the rooms that she regarded as national treasures were brought back to their original glory. As officials at the John F. Kennedy Presidential Library and Museum have written, "Under her leadership, the White House became a place of pilgrimage, a place to learn about America's history and culture, a place to showcase America's heritage."

Once the restoration was completed, Mrs. Kennedy's great desire was to share it with the American public. And she was aware that the best way to do that was through television. The result was a groundbreaking televised tour of the White House.

On the evening of February 14, 1962, *A Tour of the White House with Mrs. John F. Kennedy* was broadcast. With the grace and eloquence that had come to characterize her, the First Lady took Americans room by room throughout the Executive Mansion, giving its history and describing how it had been restored. The program not only delighted viewers but attracted a record audience of several hundred million around the globe, making it one of the most-watched programs of what would become known as television's "golden era." But the First Lady derived the greatest satisfaction from the letters more than ten thousand children wrote to her, thanking her for making the White House beautiful again.

ABOVE: Jacqueline Kennedy's knowledge and appreciation of art helped her greatly with her White House restoration. In this photograph she is being shown paintings by Charles Bird King, an artist renowned for his depictions of Native Americans.

OPPOSITE: Television cameras follow Jacqueline's every move as she describes renovations made to the White House State Dining Room during her historic TV tour.

THE PRESIDENT'S PHOTOGRAPHER

"The highest duty of . . . the artist is to remain true to himself and to let the chips fall where they may. In serving his vision of the truth, the artist best serves his nation."

Before John Kennedy became president, photography had little to do with defining the public and private image of the nation's chief executive. But all that changed when thousands of pictures demystified the public and personal life of the first family.

The person most responsible for bringing about this important change was an army photographer named Cecil Stoughton. During World War II, Stoughton served as a combat photographer in the South Pacific. The

turning point in his career came when the army assigned him to take pictures during the many festivities connected with John Kennedy's inauguration. Kennedy was so pleased with Stoughton's photographs, he had him appointed the nation's first official White House photographer. The appointment gave Stoughton the unprecedented opportunity to record the life of a president. He would take more than twelve thousand photographs, many of which would be circulated throughout the world.

While Kennedy fully appreciated the importance of the photographs Stoughton was taking, his energetic nature often made the photographer's work extremely challenging. Stoughton was always aware that he would probably have time for only one or two snaps of his camera before the president would go striding off to his next activity.

Of all the photographs that Stoughton took during the Kennedy years, the picture on the opposite page was his personal favorite. "One day I was just sitting outside the President's office," he later said, "and I heard all this noise and he waved me in. The children were dancing in the Oval Office and the President was clapping. . . . I snapped twelve frames. That afternoon the President flipped through the pictures and chose one to send to the press—it showed up in every metropolitan daily in the U.S. and around the world."

He was not a government official, a politician, or a statesman. But through his photographs, Cecil Stoughton played an important role in helping to shape an era.

ABOVE: Cecil Stoughton aboard the USS *Joseph P. Kennedy Jr.* in 1962.

OPPOSITE: John Kennedy's Oval Office reflected his love of naval history. On the walls were pictures of famous naval battles. The swords hanging above John-John's head belonged to John Barry, considered to be the father of the United States Navy.

MEET THE PRESS

"Truth is a tyrant—the only tyrant to whom we can give our allegiance. The service of truth is a matter of heroism."

No American president had ever had a better understanding of the press than John Kennedy. He was a voracious reader and pored over several newspapers a day. He was acquainted with the newsmen and newswomen who covered the White House; he knew their special needs, their likes and dislikes, and the pressures they faced to meet their deadlines.

Most American presidents were not fond of news conferences. They were concerned that they would be asked questions they could not answer, or would accidentally make statements that would turn out to be false. Many tried to hold as few press conferences as possible. Kennedy, on the other hand, relished them. He welcomed the opportunity to express his views on subjects he felt were important to the nation. He looked forward to the exchanges he had with the reporters.

Through his numerous news conferences, Kennedy displayed how he was able to use the media to shape his presidency. He was in office for little more than a thousand days, yet in that relatively short period of time, he held sixty-four news briefings. The first of these, held less than a week after he became president, drew a television audience of some sixty-five million people.

Kennedy carried out these news briefings so effectively that, in a national poll conducted in 1962, an amazing 91 percent of those surveyed stated that they were impressed with the way he responded to reporters' questions. It was surely due to his wit, intelligence, and, most important, his understanding and command of the issues. And there was another reason as well. "We citizens may rejoice," wrote *Washington Post* reporter Rowland Evans Jr., "that the President possesses the genius of humor. In that place which he occupies, in these times of high danger and awful responsibilities, humor is indeed the saving grace."

ABOVE: In response to John Kennedy's innovation of holding live television press conferences, the Radio and Television Executives Society presented him with this medal for "Outstanding Contribution to Broadcasting."

OPPOSITE: John Kennedy calls on a reporter during one of his many press conferences. No president has ever welcomed these exchanges with the press more than Kennedy.

COVERING THE WHITE HOUSE

"In a time of turbulence and change, it is more true than ever that knowledge is power."

Freedom of the press is protected by the U.S. Bill of Rights because it is considered one of the essential building blocks of a democratic society and one of the greatest safeguards of liberty. Along with this freedom comes the responsibility for journalists to report the news as accurately and fairly as possible. It is an awesome duty, for, as renowned journalist Walter Lippmann wrote, "Without criticism and reliable and intelligent reporting, the government cannot govern."

This responsibility falls heavily upon the members of the White House press corps—the journalists whose job it is to inform the American public of the president's daily activities and his position on the vital issues of the day. The White House press secretary, a position established by Herbert Hoover in 1929, is the president's

spokesperson. The press secretary holds a daily press briefing and occasional press conferences for the press corps to keep them up-to-date on all news and to answer their questions.

John Kennedy's press secretary, Pierre Salinger, became an editor for the *San Francisco Chronicle* at the age of twenty-one. Kennedy used to refer to Salinger as "the voice of the White House." He played an important role in Kennedy's handling of the Cuban Missile Crisis, controlling information for national security purposes while updating and reassuring a frightened public. Of that time, Salinger said, "The next six days were the most anxious and active of my life."

ABOVE: March 30, 1981, was one of the darkest days in the history of the press corps. President Reagan's press secretary, James S. Brady, was shot during an assassination attempt on the president's life, which left him with permanent brain damage. Police officer Thomas Delahanty was also wounded.

OPPOSITE: In the days before e-mail or cell phones, the sight of White House reporters inside telephone booths, hastily calling in their stories to their newspapers or magazines, was a daily occurrence.

A PRESIDENT ON THE MOVE

"[The president] is the vital center of action in our whole scheme of government."

White House photographer Cecil Stoughton was hardly the only person close to John Kennedy to note that the restless president was always on the go, always moving from one important meeting to another, continuously dealing with a never-ending array of domestic and foreign issues and crises and challenges. "When you are around here," presidential staff member Major General Ted Clifton remembers Kennedy remarking, "you have to eat fast, read fast, think fast, and sleep fast or else you won't get anything done."

John Kennedy could certainly read fast, an astounding twelve hundred words a minute. And despite the back injury that kept him continually in a brace and often on crutches when he was out of public view, he maintained a daily schedule that would have worn out most mortals. After following Kennedy around on one of the president's typical days, *New York Times* reporter James Reston wrote, "He did everything today except shinny up the Washington Monument."

Previous presidents had had airplanes dedicated to their use. But Kennedy was determined to have an aircraft more suitable to take him safely and swiftly to the places he needed to get to around the world. Moreover, he wanted a plane that would provide him and his staff with offices, conference rooms, sleeping quarters, and a communications system that would enable them to carry on their work no matter how far they traveled. By this time, the jet engine had been invented and airliners were bigger than ever. On Kennedy's orders, a huge, jet-powered Boeing 707 was secured for his use and modified to enable him to take almost all of the Oval Office staff with him while in flight. Today, an even larger and more sophisticated plane, a Boeing 747, remains the president's aircraft, the most photographed airplane in the world.

ABOVE: John Kennedy holds a meeting with his aides aboard Air Force One. The communications system on the aircraft is one of the most technologically advanced in the world.

OPPOSITE: Whenever the president flies in an air force jet, it is called Air Force One. Today, Air Force One has four thousand square feet of interior floor space, including two galleys that can provide a hundred meals at one sitting.

A YOUNG FIRST FAMILY

"Children are the world's most valuable resource and its best hope for the future."

By the time he entered the White House, John Kennedy had become the father of two children: Caroline, who was three, and John Jr.—or John-John, as his father was fond of calling him—who was two months. They were the first small children of a president to move into the White House since Theodore Roosevelt's family, and their presence, combined with the energy of their parents, brought a youthful spirit to the White House that captivated the nation.

Long after the Kennedy years in the White House were over, Cecil Stoughton would proclaim that his greatest joys while serving as the president's photographer took place when he was photographing Caroline and John-John. "I never made a bad picture of the children," he later stated. "You couldn't. All you had to do was aim the camera and shoot. You always got something. I became such a part of the scene that many times I didn't even need a telephoto lens. I was close enough just to take pictures normally. And they expected it."

The photographs of the Kennedy children not only delighted the public but added immeasurably to the appeal and popularity of their father. "The President," Stoughton later stated in an interview, "really benefited from his youth and the children factor—I mean, you never saw [President Herbert] Hoover or [President Franklin] Roosevelt playing on the floor with their kids. Pictures of President Kennedy bouncing the children on his knee or playing the drums with them made him appear human."

ABOVE: Caroline always made a funny face whenever she saw Stoughton coming, as she's doing in this photo with her cousin Maria Shriver. He'd coax her into a more natural pose by saying, "Now let's make one for your Mommy."

OPPOSITE: The delight that John Kennedy took in his children is obvious in this photograph, taken after they interrupted his work to show off their Halloween costumes.

IN SERVICE TO AMERICA

"I can imagine no place where you can use your powers more fully . . . in the 1960s than to be in the service of the United States."

Although he had been raised in a wealthy family, John Kennedy grew up with a deep sense of obligation to help those who were less privileged than he. His inaugural address had been a call for national service, and only six weeks after he took office he launched a program that would become an enduring legacy of his administration. It was called the Peace Corps, and it inspired young people throughout the nation.

Kennedy first articulated the idea of the Peace Corps in the final weeks of his presidential election campaign. In a speech he gave at the University of Michigan, he challenged students to become ambassadors of goodwill by volunteering to live and work in underdeveloped countries around the world. There they would, among other tasks, teach various needed skills, provide medical assistance, and build roads, bridges, and homes.

In the fall of 1961, five hundred volunteers became the first Peace Corps workers to be sent abroad. Less than two years later, their ranks had swelled to more than five thousand. The stated goals of the Corps were to bring aid to people in need, to introduce these people to Americans, and to introduce young Americans to people in distant lands. But Kennedy had an unstated goal as well. From the beginning, he saw the Peace Corps as an important vehicle for conveying the benefits of freedom and democracy to nations whose own citizens had been denied these rights.

Much to the president's satisfaction, the Peace Corps was a great success. And it brought about a development at home that exceeded even Kennedy's hopes. During the decade before Kennedy was elected, college students in general had become disinterested in government service. Newspapers had labeled them "the silent generation." By 1963, however, a poll of college campuses revealed that students regarded the Peace Corps as the nation's "most admired institution," and the number of college graduates applying for civil service jobs had increased as never before.

ABOVE: President Kennedy greets more than six hundred Peace Corps volunteers training for overseas assignments. He congratulated them on having "committed themselves to a great adventure" and hoped that when their assignments were completed, they would return to careers of service in the government.

OPPOSITE: One of the underlying goals of the Peace Corps was to help people, particularly young people, in disadvantaged lands learn to help themselves. Here, a Peace Corps volunteer shows a Guatemalan youngster how to plant trees native to his country.

AN IDOL OF YOUTH

*"We have the power to make this the best generation ...
in the history of the world—or to make it the last."*

*J*ohn Kennedy's vitality, his own relative youth, and his inspiring messages made him extraordinarily popular with young people throughout the world. In this unique picture, White House photographer Cecil Stoughton captured the scene as an enormous crowd of admiring high school students from fifty-six countries gathered on the White House lawn to "meet" the president. The young people were spending a year studying in the United States.

Kennedy

A RACE FOR SPACE

"I believe that this nation should commit itself to achieving the goal, before this decade is out, of landing a man on the moon and returning him safely to the earth."

The struggle between Russia and the United States for military superiority and the cooperation of other nations would, more than any other issue, occupy John Kennedy's attention during his time in the White House. Some three years before Kennedy took office, Russia launched an earth-orbiting artificial satellite named *Sputnik I*—taking the cold war into space. Then, less than three months into Kennedy's presidency, the Soviet Union scored an even greater triumph when cosmonaut Yuri Gagarin made a complete orbit of the earth and became the first person to enter space.

On May 5, 1961, the United States responded when Alan Shepard became the first American to be launched into space. Compared to Gagarin's achievement, Shepard's suborbital flight was a modest accomplishment. But then John Kennedy made a startling announcement: his ultimate goal was to put an American on the moon before the 1960s were over.

For many, Kennedy's goal seemed impossible. But on February 20, 1962, America took a giant step forward when John Glenn orbited the earth three times. The nation was overjoyed, but Kennedy knew there was still much to be done before we reached the moon. Seven years later, thanks to American ingenuity and determination, the "impossible" was achieved.

Kennedy would not live to see his goal fulfilled. He would not be alive on July 20, 1969, when six hundred million people around the world were glued to their television sets to see astronaut Neil Armstrong become the first person to step on the lunar surface. But one thing was clear: it was John Kennedy's vision, daring, and commitment that had made one of humanity's boldest dreams a reality.

ABOVE: The first human to orbit the earth, Yuri Gagarin became one of the world's greatest celebrities. He was made a high Russian official and also worked on designs for improved spacecraft before his death in a plane crash at age thirty-four.

OPPOSITE: John Glenn shows President Kennedy the inside of the space capsule *Friendship 7*. Glenn's flight, which orbited the earth, moved the United States closer to fulfilling Kennedy's goal of landing a man on the moon.

SHAPING UP AMERICA

"We do not want our children to become a generation of spectators. Rather, we want each of them to be a participant in the vigorous life."

As a U.S. senator, John Kennedy had been disturbed by research showing that potential American military recruits were being rejected at an alarming rate as physically unfit for duty. Another study revealed that each year more than twice the number of American children failed physical fitness tests as did European youngsters.

Shortly after being elected president, Kennedy did something no other president-elect had ever done—he published an article in a national magazine describing a program he intended to introduce. Titled "The Soft American," the *Sports Illustrated* article stressed the importance of physical fitness as a "foundation for

the vigor and vitality of all the activities of the nation." Outlining the problem, Kennedy stated, "There is . . . an increasingly large number of young Americans . . . whose physical fitness is not what it should be—who are getting soft." This softness, he proclaimed, "will destroy much of our ability to meet the great and vital challenges which confront our people. . . . Now it is time," he declared, "for the United States to move forward with a national program to improve the fitness of all Americans."

Putting his words into action, Kennedy built upon a physical fitness program established by his predecessor, Dwight D. Eisenhower, by targeting the nation's youth. Physical fitness awareness even became the theme of many comic strips, including the highly popular *Peanuts*, whose character Snoopy often encouraged youngsters to do their "daily dozen" exercises. Probably the most unusual item in the fitness program was the specially created "Chicken Fat Song," whose humorous lyrics led schoolchildren through a rigorous exercise routine.

Kennedy's program was a great success. By the end of its first year, 50 percent more American students passed a national physical fitness test than had passed a year earlier. Just as encouraging, schools around the country began placing greater emphasis on physical education programs.

ABOVE: The Kennedy family always emphasized the importance of an active life. Here, John appears on a youth football team (bottom row, far right). His love of sports continued in the legendary touch-football games the family competed in at their Hyannis Port compound.

OPPOSITE: The front cover of the exercise book that was part of Kennedy's physical fitness program. As the line above the title states, the book was a huge success around the globe.

U.S. OFFICIAL PHYSICAL FITNESS PROGRAM

A fitness program for all that takes only a few minutes a day

PREPARED BY
THE PRESIDENT'S COUNCIL ON PHYSICAL FITNESS

DIRECTED BY BUD WILKINSON

A SPECIAL PROGRAM

"We can say with some assurance that, although children may be the victims of fate, they will not be the victims of our neglect."

John Kennedy and his brothers were not alone in dedicating themselves to service for others. Their sister Eunice Kennedy Shriver made an important contribution to aiding a large and special segment of the world's population. Like her brother John, Eunice was close to their sister Rosemary, who was intellectually disabled. Undoubtedly their relationship was a major factor in Eunice's 1968 establishment of an organization called Special Olympics, dedicated to helping people with intellectual disabilities become physically fit, gain greater self-confidence, and become respected members of their communities.

It was a wonderful idea, but even Eunice could not have foreseen where it would lead. Today, Special Olympics serves more than 3.1 million people in over two hundred countries throughout the world. Impressive numbers, but even more important is the way that Special Olympics training and competition in thirty different sports has helped millions of people, many of whom were formerly isolated and unappreciated, find an avenue to self-fulfillment and acceptance.

Thanks to what she founded and devoted much of her life to, Eunice Kennedy Shriver was inducted into the National Women's Hall of Fame and awarded the 1984 Presidential Medal of Freedom. When she died in August 2009, the church holding her funeral overflowed with children who were part of the Special Olympics program. Letters thanking her for what she had created poured in from around the world. All were fitting tributes to a woman who saw a special need and filled it in a very special way.

ABOVE: Despite being born to wealth and privilege, Eunice Kennedy Shriver, like most of her brothers and sisters, devoted her life to public service.

OPPOSITE (TOP): Special Olympics operates at local, national, and international levels. Here, as an enormous crowd looks on, participants in the 2003 Special Olympics World Games enter the stadium in Croke Park, Dublin, Ireland, for the event's opening ceremony.

OPPOSITE (BOTTOM): Special Olympics has opened a whole new world to intellectually disabled individuals. Here, a woman cheers on a Special Olympics athlete as she competes in a race.

CANDID PHOTOGRAPHY

"I have a nice home, the office is close by, and the pay is good."

Smaller, lighter, easier-to-use cameras were a major factor in photography's coming-of-age in the 1950s and early '60s. With the invention of film that enabled pictures to be taken in rapid-fire sequence, a new approach to the medium quickly gained popularity: candid photography.

A candid photograph is one that is unposed or natural. The picture on this page of John Kennedy caught unaware by the camera while enjoying an ice cream cone is a prime example not only of a candid photograph but of the often charming nature of such unposed images.

It was during the Kennedy years that candid photography truly came into its own. The nation's magazines and newspapers competed with each other for informal pictures to satisfy Americans' seemingly insatiable appetite—Jacqueline on horseback, Caroline in her tree house, or John-John suddenly appearing in the Oval Office during one of his father's meetings with aides or foreign dignitaries. Particularly popular were pictures of the first family sailing or cavorting on the beach at the summer White House at Hyannis Port, or of the president engaged in a spirited game of touch football with his brothers and friends.

Among the most memorable candid images is the one on the opposite page. Cecil Stoughton came upon one of Caroline's ponies, named Leprechaun, nibbling on her father's ear as a family friend tried to get the animal to stop. As Stoughton raised his camera, Kennedy called out to him, "Keep shooting, [Stoughton], you are about to see a president being eaten by a horse."

ABOVE: Seeing Kennedy in such unguarded moments made him seem more accessible and human—and strengthened his connection with the public.

OPPOSITE: When asked which of the Kennedy family photographs were, in his opinion, most memorable, Cecil Stoughton said the ones that were not posed—pictures that nobody could plan or predict.

FAILURE AT THE BAY OF PIGS

"There's an old saying that victory has a hundred fathers and defeat is an orphan."

In one of his first briefings after being elected president, John Kennedy was told of a bold plan developed during the Eisenhower administration. Designed to remove Cuban leader Fidel Castro from power and replace him with a noncommunist government friendly to the United States, the plan called for an invasion of Cuba at a coastal area known as the Bay of Pigs. The attack was to be carried out by Cuban exiles who had been secretly trained in invasion tactics by the American Central Intelligence Agency (CIA).

It would turn into a major disaster. The American bombers sent to destroy Cuba's air force while most of its planes were on the ground failed to hit their targets. Worse yet, Castro had learned of the impending attack and had placed twenty thousand troops on the beaches to repel the assault. When the attack took place on April 17, 1961, the invaders were first shot at from above by the Cuban planes that had not been destroyed and then soundly defeated by the waiting Cuban ground troops. More than one hundred invaders were killed and some twelve hundred others were forced to surrender.

The disaster would have widespread effects. Not only would it cause John Kennedy great embarrassment, it would convince Russian leader Nikita Khrushchev that the American president was weak enough to be bullied . . . and it would lead to a far greater crisis between the defenders of communism and the defenders of democracy.

ABOVE: Russian leader Nikita Khrushchev and Cuban leader Fidel Castro greet each other. Cuba's Russian-backed communist government posed a threat to all the nations in the Americas.

OPPOSITE: Like all those who have held the presidency, John Kennedy experienced many moments of deep concern and even anguish. The failure at the Bay of Pigs was a particularly troubling time for a man accustomed to success.

BRINK OF DISASTER

"When I ran for the Presidency of the United States . . . I could not realize . . . how heavy and constant would be [the] burdens."

On October 14, 1962, in yet another example of the role photography played in the life of John Kennedy, American spy planes equipped with highly sophisticated cameras captured pictures of Russian nuclear missile–launching sites being erected in communist Cuba, just ninety miles south of Florida. The ensuing Cuban Missile Crisis was, by far, the greatest challenge the young president would face, one in which the safety—perhaps even the survival—of the whole world hung in the balance.

With Russian ships, loaded with enough nuclear missiles to kill at least eighty-five million Americans, about to set sail for the missile-launching sites, Kennedy assembled his military leaders and key cabinet members and advisers. Their awesome task was to decide what to do in the face of potential nuclear war. Most of the military men and some of the advisers urged an immediate bombing of the launching sites, followed by a full-scale invasion of Cuba. Others argued that such a strategy would force the Soviet Union to retaliate, resulting in the most dangerous war in history. In the end, Kennedy decided that the best course of action was to place American warships off Cuba, in the path of the missile-carrying Russian vessels.

Then Kennedy went on the radio and on television stating, "It shall be the policy of this nation to regard any nuclear missile launched from Cuba . . . as an attack by the Soviet Union on the United States, requiring a full retaliatory response upon the Soviet Union." For two days after Kennedy's remarks, the world—closer to nuclear war than at any time in history—held its breath. Finally, on October 24, missile-carrying Russian ships reached the spot where the American vessels lay blocking their path—and they turned back! Four days later, Russia's leader, Nikita Khrushchev, informed Kennedy that he had "given a new order to dismantle the [missile sites]." Cooler heads had prevailed. Thanks to the leadership of John Kennedy and Nikita Khrushchev, a nuclear holocaust had been averted.

ABOVE: The doodles John Kennedy drew during one of his many Cuban Missile Crisis meetings, in which he wrote the word "decision" over and over again, reveal how he struggled to find the right course of action.

OPPOSITE: The information provided by cameras aboard American spy planes provided indisputable proof of the missile launchers and related equipment that the Russians were erecting in Cuba.

MRBM FIELD LAUNCH SITE
SAN CRISTOBAL NO 1
14 OCTOBER 1962

ERECTOR/LAUNCHER EQUIPMENT

TENT AREAS

EQUIPMENT

ERECTOR/LAUNCHER EQUIPMENT

8 MISSILE TRAILERS

A VITAL SPEECH

"Freedom has many difficulties and democracy is not perfect, but we have never had to put a wall up to keep our people in."

Cuba was not the only "battleground" of the cold war. At the close of World War II, Russia had occupied the eastern part of Germany and had then erected the heavily guarded Berlin Wall, which separated communist East Berlin from noncommunist West Berlin. The people of East Berlin were not allowed to leave. The Russians didn't even permit them to visit relatives in West Berlin.

In June 1963, John Kennedy traveled to West Berlin, both to show support for the West Berliners and to affirm the United States' commitment to the freedom of all people. He was greeted by more than two million West Berliners who lined the streets, eager to hear him speak. His speech, attended by some one hundred fifty thousand people, would rank among the most memorable he would ever deliver.

Standing in the shadow of the Berlin Wall, he declared, "There are many people in the world who really don't understand, or say they don't, what is the great issue between the free world and the communist world. Let them come to Berlin. There are some who say that communism is the wave of the future. Let them come to Berlin. And there are some who say in Europe and elsewhere we can work with the communists. Let them come to Berlin. And there are even a few who say that it is true that communism is an evil system, but it permits us to make economic progress. . . . Let them come to Berlin."

Each statement was greeted with an enormous roar of approval from the West Berliners. But the loudest cheer of all came when Kennedy affirmed his belief that the West Berliners were giving the world a lesson in democracy: "As a free man, I take pride in the words, *'Ich bin ein Berliner* [I am a Berliner].'" It had been such a triumphant speech that when Kennedy left Germany, he turned to an aide and said, "We'll never have another day like this one as long as we live."

ABOVE: In this dramatic photograph, a West Berlin woman standing at the Berlin Wall raises her hands in frustration after trying for hours to be allowed to enter East Berlin and visit her friends and relatives.

OPPOSITE: John Kennedy delivers his inspiring speech to thousands of Berliners. "Freedom is indivisible," he told the crowd, "and when one man is enslaved, all are not free."

HOME TO IRELAND

"[Ireland] is a free country, and that is why any American feels at home."

On the same day he delivered his historic Berlin speech, Kennedy traveled to Ireland, a country he held deep in his heart. It was a special trip for a man whose family, on both his mother's and his father's sides, had deep Irish roots.

After the stress of the Cuban Missile Crisis and the drama of his trip to Berlin, Kennedy's visit was a joyous occasion from beginning to end. Treated everywhere like a returning heroic native son, he met with scores of distant relatives and toured the original family cottage. "When my great-grandfather left here to become a [barrel maker] in East Boston," he told the villagers, "he carried nothing with him except two things: a strong religious faith and a strong desire for liberty. I am glad to say that all of his great-grandchildren have valued that inheritance."

Speaking before the Irish parliament, he stated, "I am deeply honored to be your guest in a free Parliament in a free Ireland." Then, with characteristic Kennedy wit, he remarked, "If this nation had achieved its present political and economic stature a century or so ago, my great-grandfather might never have left [Ireland], and I might, if fortunate, be sitting [in this parliament] with you." He continued his remarks, reminding the Irish lawmakers that "no nation, large or small, can be indifferent to the fate of others, near or far. Modern economics, weaponry, and communications have made us all realize more than ever that we are one human family and this one planet is our home."

After the visit was over, Robert Kennedy, aware that many members of the press had questioned the value of the busy president's trip, publicly stated that his brother's Irish journey was "the happiest time of his administration."

ABOVE: During his Irish "homecoming," John Kennedy made a point of stopping to greet his well-wishers wherever he went.

OPPOSITE: John Kennedy had always publicly relished his Irish heritage, but even he was unprepared for the extraordinary welcome he received in Ireland.

A HISTORIC TREATY

"The weapons of war must be abolished before they abolish us."

The peaceful resolution of the Cuban Missile Crisis brought a collective sigh of relief from people around the world. Many regarded the event as John F. Kennedy's greatest triumph. But the president himself saw it as something more than a diplomatic victory. He regarded it as an opportunity.

From the time he became president and was briefed on the true potential for nuclear destruction, Kennedy had become determined to do what he could to end nuclear weapons testing and the buildup of nuclear arms. With the Cuban crisis behind him, Kennedy began secretly writing letters to Nikita Khrushchev, urging the Russian leader to join with him in banning all further testing of nuclear weapons. At the same time, he made a deliberate effort to change the harsh tone of his remarks concerning Russia. In a commencement speech at American University, Kennedy, speaking of the two nations, stated that "in the final analysis, our most basic common link is that we all inhabit this small planet. We all breathe the same air. We all cherish our children's future. And we are all mortal."

The address so impressed Khrushchev that he echoed Kennedy's proposal to outlaw the testing of nuclear weapons. In a radio and television address on July 26, 1963, Kennedy informed the nation, "Yesterday a shaft of light cut into the darkness. Negotiations were concluded in Moscow on a treaty to ban all nuclear tests in the atmosphere, in outer space, and under water." On August 5, 1963, the United States, the United Kingdom, and the Soviet Union signed the Nuclear Test-Ban Treaty.

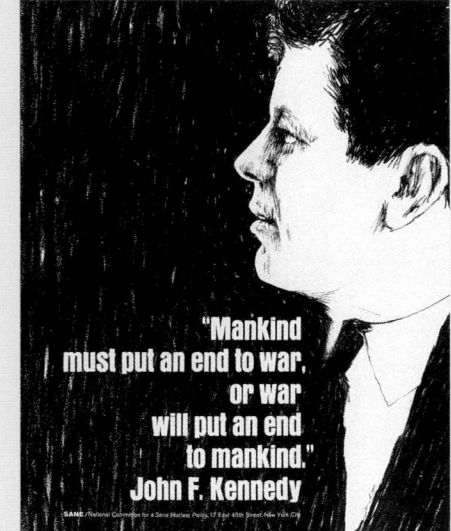

"Mankind must put an end to war, or war will put an end to mankind."
John F. Kennedy

SANE/National Committee for a Sane Nuclear Policy, 17 East 45th Street, New York City

ABOVE: Through his eloquent, often-quoted words and through achievements such as the Nuclear Test-Ban Treaty, John Kennedy demonstrated to the world what a young president could accomplish.

OPPOSITE: Kennedy signs the Nuclear Test-Ban Treaty. As he worked toward a more peaceful relationship with Russia and its leader, Nikita Khrushchev, Kennedy stated, "It is insane that two men, sitting on opposite sides of the world, should be able to decide to bring an end to civilization."

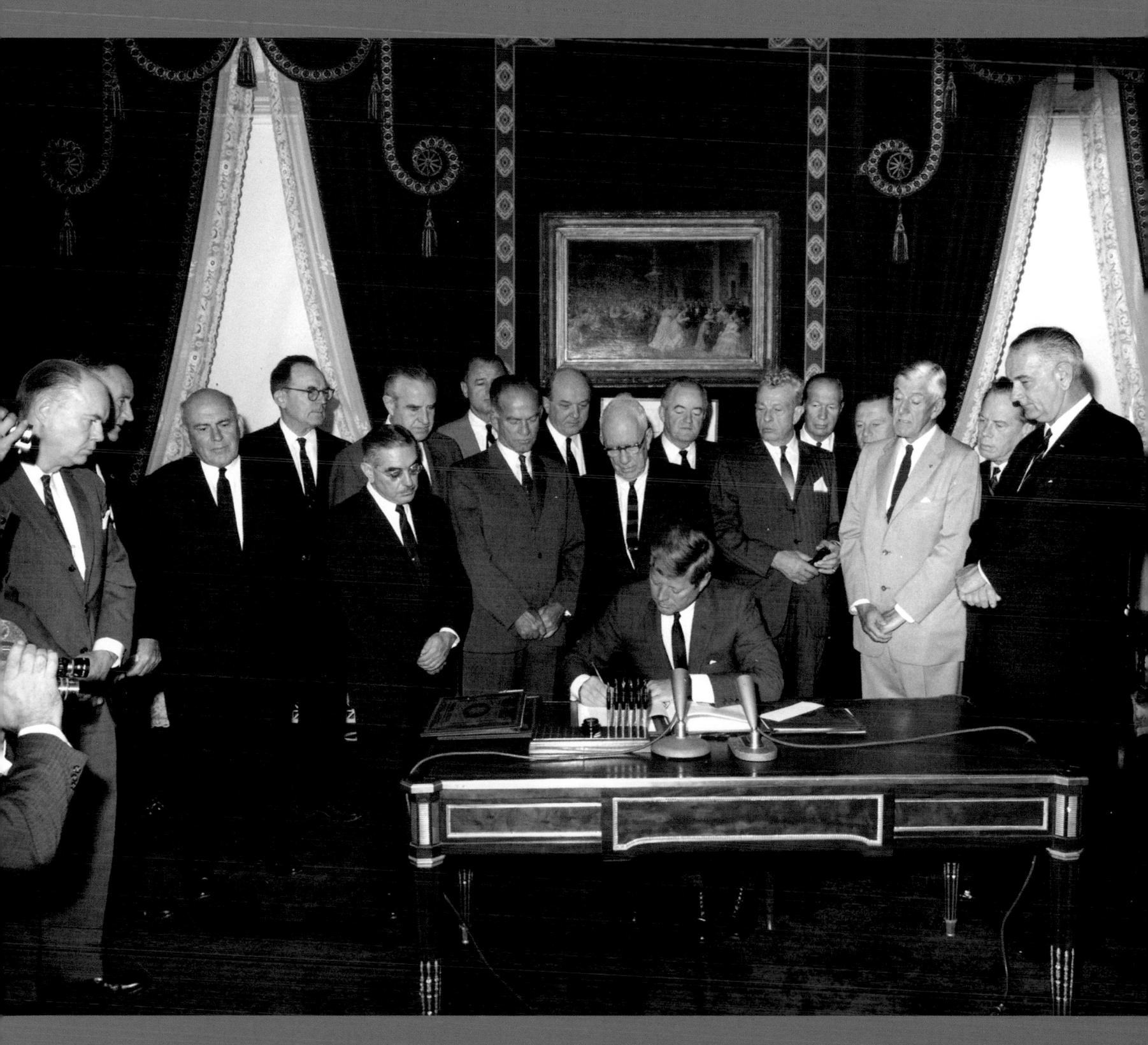

BROTHERS

"Just as I went into politics because Joe died, if anything happened to me tomorrow, my brother Bobby would run for my seat.... And if Bobby died, Teddy would take over for him."

The loss of his brother Joe Jr. in World War II was a bitter blow to John Kennedy. But he was fortunate to have two other brothers with whom he was not only close but who helped him throughout his political career. In particular, Robert Kennedy played a key role in John's campaigns for both the House of Representatives and the Senate. And Robert's nonstop efforts and his ability to persuade Democratic Party leaders to support his brother were crucial to John's winning the presidential nomination.

After the election, an even bigger role lay ahead for Robert Kennedy. Once John appointed him attorney general of the United States, he became a relentless fighter against organized crime and a passionate defender of the rights of working men and women. Robert was also his brother's most trusted adviser—especially regarding the Cuban Missile Crisis and the civil rights movement.

The youngest of the Kennedy brothers, Edward (known as Ted or Teddy) became an important political figure in his own right. When, at the age of thirty, he was elected to the United States Senate in 1962, his opponents charged that he won the seat only because of the Kennedy name. But despite this criticism and several personal scandals, Ted Kennedy worked for more than forty-six years to become one of the most productive and respected senators in the nation's history. Many historians, in fact, regard him as the most effective senator the United States has ever had.

In 1968, Robert Kennedy—who, four years earlier, had been elected senator from New York—was tragically assassinated while carrying out his own campaign for the presidency. Ted Kennedy died of a brain tumor in 2009.

ABOVE: John Kennedy was always close to his brothers. Here, Edward sits on the future president's shoulders while Robert poses in front of him.

OPPOSITE: Robert, Edward, and John Kennedy ponder a difficult problem. All three devoted their adult lives to government service and to one another.

A GROUNDBREAKING CONFRONTATION

"One hundred years of delay have passed since President Lincoln freed the slaves, yet their heirs... are not yet freed from the bonds of injustice."

While the cold war raged internationally, the 1960s also saw great turmoil within the United States. Throughout the South, African Americans were denied access to public places and the right to register to vote. And despite a Supreme Court ruling desegregating public schools, most Southern states refused to obey the law. As a result, African Americans and their supporters staged marches, demonstrations, sit-ins, and other forms of protest. Many African American leaders were critical of the president, feeling that Kennedy had not actively used the power of his office to correct these injustices. Kennedy, however, aware of how politically explosive the race issue was in the North as well as the South, felt he needed to move slowly.

Then, on June 11, 1963, an event took place that profoundly affected both Kennedy and the civil rights movement. As two African American students attempted to enroll at the University of Alabama, the state's governor, George Wallace, stood in a doorway blocking their way. Outraged at Wallace's action, Kennedy sent federal marshals to demand Wallace allow the black students to enter. Wallace, however, still refused to budge, forcing Kennedy to federalize the Alabama National Guard. Finally Wallace stepped aside, and the two students entered the building and enrolled.

The confrontation was a turning point for Kennedy. That evening in a television and radio address to the nation, he announced he was sending a bill to Congress asking it to enact laws that would give African Americans the right "to receive equal service in places... such as hotels and restaurants and theaters and retail stores" and the right "to register to vote... without interference or fear of reprisal."

For Kennedy, it was a proud moment. "Sometimes," he told a friend, "you look at what you've done and the only thing you ask yourself is, 'What took you so long to do it?'"

ABOVE: John Kennedy meets with leaders of the African American civil rights movement. Kennedy's civil rights bill thrilled most of these leaders, many of whom thought he had taken too long to use his power to advance their cause.

OPPOSITE: In attempting to prevent African American students from enrolling at the University of Alabama, Governor George Wallace carried out his vow of "segregation today... segregation tomorrow... segregation forever."

A HISTORIC MARCH

"It ought to be possible... for every American to enjoy the privileges of being American without regard to his race or his color."

Throughout the history of the United States there have been many political rallies, but none has been more influential than the March on Washington for Jobs and Freedom that took place on August 28, 1963. One major purpose of the event was to show support for the civil rights legislation John Kennedy had proposed to Congress. Many who took part in the march, however, did so to demand even stronger measures than Kennedy had proposed—especially legislation that would result in more jobs for African Americans.

Even the march's organizers could not have anticipated the number of people who converged on Washington. Traveling in more than two thousand buses, twenty-one special trains, ten chartered airplanes, and thousands of cars, more than two hundred fifty thousand people marched from the Washington Monument to the Lincoln Memorial for a program of music and speakers. Nor could anyone have predicted the enormous media coverage the event would elicit. More television cameras were used than had filmed John Kennedy's inauguration.

Among those who sang in the shadow of the Lincoln Memorial were famed gospel singer Mahalia Jackson and popular folk singers Joan Baez and Bob Dylan. The highlight of the event was the speech given by the great African American leader Dr. Martin Luther King Jr. It was in this speech that Dr. King spoke the now-immortal line, "I have a dream that my four little children will one day live in a nation where they will not be judged by the color of their skin but by the content of their character."

The March on Washington was a pivotal development in the civil rights movement; it is widely credited as being instrumental in passing the Civil Rights Act in 1964 and the National Voting Rights Act in 1965.

ABOVE: Dr. Martin Luther King Jr. was one of the greatest orators of the twentieth century. His words inspired not only those involved in the American civil rights movement but individuals everywhere dedicated to freedom and equality for all people.

OPPOSITE: The enormous crowd that attended the March on Washington for Jobs and Freedom stretched as far as the eye could see. Far in the background of this photograph is the Washington Monument.

A MAN OF THE SEA

"We are tied to the ocean. And when we go back to the sea, whether it is to sail or to watch it we are going back from whence we came."

As the leader of the "free world," John Kennedy had enormous pressures placed upon him. Fortunately, although the opportunities were all too few, there were ways he could relax. He loved to read; even if he was too busy to enjoy a book from cover to cover, he did find time to read at least a few pages for pleasure every day.

Kennedy also loved movies. Whether he was in the White House or in the family's summer retreat on Cape Cod, he watched a movie every night he could—particularly Westerns and other films that allowed him to escape from the problems of the day.

The president's physical activities were limited by his back problems, but when he felt up to it, he loved

to play a few holes of golf. Ever a perfectionist—and aware of the advantages of a personal cameraman—he had Cecil Stoughton photograph his golf swing and putting stroke so a professional could analyze them and tell him how he could improve his game.

Most of all, he relaxed by being next to or on the sea, particularly on Cape Cod. He needed the Cape, he said, "to feel the salt in my face." Whether it was helping Caroline maneuver her remote-controlled sailboat, playing on the beach with John-John, or swimming in the waters off the family compound, nothing restored his energy or relaxed his mind more than the Cape Cod sun and sea. And nothing pleased him more than cruising Cape Cod's waters.

He enjoyed puttering around on his old sailboat *The Victura*, but for him the ultimate pleasure was sitting back in his special swivel chair aboard the much larger vessel the *Honey Fitz*, surrounded by friends and family and, for a short time, leaving his responsibilities ashore. More than any other president, John F. Kennedy was truly a man of the sea.

ABOVE: In a rare unguarded moment, John Kennedy relaxes by reading a magazine while spending the day at sea.

OPPOSITE: As he grew older, Edward Kennedy (left) became an accomplished sailor, thanks largely to the expert instruction he received from his older brother John.

KENNEDY'S SECRETS

"The doctors...tell me I'll probably last until I'm forty-five."

It was ironic. Thanks to the enormous exposure that television and photography brought him, John Kennedy was the most public president the nation had ever had. At the same time, the media observed an unwritten rule that a president's private life was off-limits and to be kept secret. That is why Kennedy's several extramarital affairs went unreported—including alleged affairs with famous movie star Marilyn Monroe and a Mafia kingpin's mistress.

There was another secret as well. John Kennedy was far more ill than the public ever knew. As a young boy and teen, Kennedy suffered so many childhood illnesses, his family often joked that if a mosquito bit him, it would surely die. And he'd so long been plagued by back problems that Robert Kennedy said, "At least one half of the days that [my brother John] spent on this earth were days of intense physical pain."

But what the public never knew was that by the time he was thirty, John Kennedy had developed a condition so serious that, when he collapsed on a visit to London in 1947, his doctor proclaimed, "He hasn't got a year to live." The same doctor, and eventually other medical specialists, diagnosed Kennedy's condition as Addison's disease—a disorder that occurs when the adrenal glands do not produce enough of certain hormones.

If Kennedy had contracted the disease only a few years earlier, he almost certainly would have died from it. Fortunately, by the time he was diagnosed, injections and drugs had been developed to help keep the illness in check. For the rest of his life, Kennedy would have to rely on heavy doses of these medications to stay alive. This life-threatening condition affected his already weakened back to the extent that, when out of the public eye, he often had to use crutches to get around.

To his credit, Kennedy never allowed his physical condition to negatively affect the way he ran his presidency. And the image of vitality that he projected largely deflected any questions that some might have raised about his health. Still, one wonders: how long would John Kennedy have lived if he had not been assassinated?

ABOVE: Despite the many ailments from which he suffered, John Kennedy always presented a vigorous, buoyant image to the public.

OPPOSITE: More than the public ever realized, John was often in physical pain. He frequently needed crutches to help him meet his demanding schedule.

UNANSWERED QUESTIONS

"Should I become your president . . . I will not risk American lives . . . by permitting any other nation to drag us into the wrong war at the wrong place and at the wrong time."

When John Kennedy took office, few Americans had ever heard of South or North Vietnam, let alone knew where they were. Yet these two adjoining Asian countries presented him with another challenge in his battle against the spread of communism. As communist North Vietnam took aim at noncommunist South Vietnam, Kennedy was faced with a dilemma: should he send in military troops to help prevent the North Vietnamese takeover, or should he keep the United States out of the conflict?

Kennedy's decision was to send thousands of military advisers to help South Vietnam prepare for its own defense. "To introduce . . . U.S. [combat] forces . . . there today," he stated, ". . . would almost certainly lead to adverse political and in the long run adverse military consequences." He was right. As Kennedy's successors Lyndon Johnson and Richard Nixon discovered to their dismay, involving the United States militarily in the Vietnam War meant becoming embroiled in a conflict that could not be won and that would bitterly divide the American people.

In the final months of his life, Kennedy held out against sending combat troops to Vietnam. Against mounting pressure, however, he refused to remove the military advisers.

All of this has led to intense debate among historians and political experts. Had he lived, would Kennedy have fully involved the United States in the Vietnam War? Or, recognizing the quagmire that the war could well become, would he have pulled the United States completely out of the conflict? They are questions that will never be answered.

Above: An American soldier sets fire to a North Vietnamese base camp. The Vietnam conflict, waged by John Kennedy's successors, would prove one of the most unpopular wars in United States history.

Opposite: Kennedy displays a map of North and South Vietnam as he explains the long, troubled history of that region and why he is sending military advisers to help stop North Vietnamese aggression.

COMMUNIST REBEL AREAS
22 MARCH 1961
COMMUNIST CHINA
NORTH VIETNAM
HANOI
LUANG PRABANG
THAILAND
LAOS
ROADS
150

A NATIONAL TRAGEDY

"A nation reveals itself not only by the men it produces but also by the men it honors, the men it remembers."

By the fall of 1963, John Kennedy and his aides were beginning to prepare for his reelection campaign in 1964, confident that, given his great popularity, the president would be reelected by a comfortable margin. They were certain also that, in the next four years, Kennedy would complete a hugely successful presidency by building upon what he had already achieved and the programs he had started.

Then, early in the fall, he accepted an invitation to speak in Dallas, Texas. Immediately, those around him became alarmed and urged the president to cancel his appearance. Many in Dallas had shown themselves to be hostile to Kennedy's programs, particularly those involving civil rights and attempts to build better relations with Russia. Only a month before, Kennedy's United Nation's ambassador, Adlai Stevenson, had been physically threatened when he had given a speech in Dallas.

Despite the concerns for his safety, the president insisted on honoring his commitment, and when he arrived in Texas on the morning of November 22, he was in typical good humor. After delivering an inspiring speech to a huge, enthusiastic crowd in Fort Worth, he was off to Dallas to ride in a motorcade to the Trade Mart, where he would deliver his major address. Because the weather was beautiful, the bulletproof bubble had been removed from the presidential car so that the thousands lining the streets could better see the president.

At about 12:30 p.m., as the motorcade passed the Texas School Book Depository, shots suddenly rang out from one of the building's windows. One bullet struck the president in the neck. Another crushed his skull. Although the presidential car sped off to a hospital close by, nothing could be done to save John Kennedy's life. At the age of forty-six, the youngest president the United States had ever elected was dead.

ABOVE: In a photograph that captures a happy moment shortly before the lives of John and Jacqueline Kennedy turned to tragedy, the president and First Lady arrive in Dallas, Texas.

OPPOSITE: Onlooker Mary Moorman's Polaroid photograph of John Kennedy's assassination was taken only one-sixth of a second after the president was shot in the head.

A MOST IMPORTANT PHOTOGRAPH

The picture on the opposite page, taken by Cecil Stoughton, has become one of the world's best-known photographs. In accordance with United States law, as soon as John Kennedy was officially pronounced dead, Vice President Lyndon B. Johnson needed to be sworn in as quickly as possible as the nation's new president. The Secret Service insisted Johnson be flown back immediately to the nation's capital, where his safety would be best assured. And so it was aboard Air Force One, before it took off for Washington, that one of the saddest swearings-in of a new American president took place.

Stoughton, the only photographer present on the plane, almost missed taking the picture. Standing on a couch at the back of the aircraft, he pressed the shutter on his camera—but nothing happened. Only after shaking it as hard as he could was he able to get it to work. The image he captured showed a somber Johnson taking the oath, flanked by his wife and by Jacqueline Kennedy, obviously and understandably in shock. The picture also shows the hastily summoned Texas federal judge, Sarah T. Hughes, the only woman ever to have sworn in a United States president, administering the oath of office.

Aside from providing the only visual record of Lyndon Johnson's swearing-in, Stoughton's photograph gave the world a vital lesson in the nature of American democracy. The picture supplied the evidence that, unlike numerous other countries in similar circumstances, there had been a peaceful transition of power. As *Life* magazine's Bobbi Baker-Burrows would later write, "At a traumatic time, in a single photograph, [Stoughton] provided the essential evidence of the continuity of government. In the confusion that followed the assassination, his photograph told the world that there was a new president, and the country that it was safe."

ABOVE: Robert Kennedy supports Jacqueline as they watch John Kennedy's coffin being removed from Air Force One and brought to a waiting ambulance.

OPPOSITE: In order to assure people that the United States government was functioning despite the horrific act that had taken place, the photograph of Lyndon Johnson's swearing-in was sent immediately around the world.

A NATION MOURNS TOGETHER

There have been events in the nation's history so traumatic, so momentous, that most people remember exactly where they were when they first heard about them. The destruction of the World Trade Center on September 11, 2001, was such an event. So too was the assassination of John F. Kennedy.

It was a time of extraordinary grief, a time when a stunned nation tried to cope with what had happened so suddenly and unexpectedly. America turned to Jacqueline Kennedy, a widow at the age of thirty-four, who gained the respect and admiration of the entire world through the courage and dignity she displayed in the assassination's aftermath.

Jacqueline made certain that her husband would be honored and properly remembered by planning every aspect of his solemn state funeral. As millions of television viewers around the world looked on, they witnessed proceedings that Mrs. Kennedy modeled directly after Abraham Lincoln's funeral. As with Lincoln, a horse-drawn, two-wheeled military vehicle called a caisson carried the slain president's casket to the White House, where more than two hundred fifty thousand people would view it as John Kennedy lay in state.

The Kennedy family had expressed their desire to have the president buried in the family plot in Brookline, Massachusetts. But Jacqueline was firm in her decision to have her husband interred in the national cemetery in Arlington, Virginia. Her reason was simply expressed. "He belongs," she stated, "to the country."

ABOVE: John-John salutes his father's coffin as the caisson carrying it passes by. This poignant photograph touched the hearts of people around the world.

OPPOSITE: Jacqueline Kennedy, flanked by Robert and Edward Kennedy, leads the funeral procession for her martyred husband. They are followed by leaders of nations around the world who came to Washington to pay their respects to the fallen American leader.

SHOCKING REALITY TV

From the moment the public learned of John Kennedy's assassination, millions of Americans and countless others around the world sat glued to their TV sets. For the next week, television would bring live images of every aspect of the slain president's funeral and of related events that would remain etched in the memories of all who saw them.

Soon after Kennedy was shot, Lee Harvey Oswald, who had spent time living in the Soviet Union and then returned to the United States, was arrested as the assassin. Now the television screen was filled with live pictures of Oswald being taken to police headquarters, of officials holding up the rifle that Oswald had allegedly used. Then came the most dramatic and astounding images of all. Cameras were live as Oswald was being transferred from police headquarters to a nearby building where he was to be questioned. Suddenly, a Dallas nightclub owner named Jack Ruby appeared on the screen, approached Oswald, and shot and killed him. This was not fictionalized television drama. This was real. An already grieving worldwide TV audience could hardly believe its eyes.

With Oswald's death, many troubling questions remained. Was there more than one gunman, or had Oswald acted alone? Had he been hired by the Cuban government as revenge for the Bay of Pigs invasion? Had the Russians recruited him in retaliation for having to back down during the Cuban Missile Crisis? Had he been sent by a top Mafia boss in retribution for Kennedy's alleged affair with the mobster's girlfriend? And what about Jack Ruby? Had he acted alone seeking atonement for the loss of John Kennedy, or was he part of a conspiracy aimed at silencing Oswald? Within a week of the assassination, a commission, headed by Supreme Court Chief Justice Earl Warren, was formed to seek answers to these and other questions. In the end, the commission ruled that both Oswald and Ruby had acted alone and that there had been no conspiracy. To this day, there are many who strongly disagree with this finding.

ABOVE: Investigations by the FBI, the Dallas police department, and the Warren Commission concluded that Lee Harvey Oswald was the man who assassinated John Kennedy. Oswald, however, vehemently denied that he had been the gunman.

OPPOSITE: A Dallas police official looks on in disbelief as Jack Ruby fires the shot that killed Lee Harvey Oswald. A familiar figure in Dallas, Ruby had been allowed to breach security and enter the heavily guarded police station from which Oswald was being transferred.

CAMELOT

Beginning in his childhood, John Kennedy loved to read about history, particularly stories about real and legendary heroes. Among his favorite were legends of King Arthur and his knights of the Round Table. Kennedy was particularly fascinated with tales of Camelot, the supposed idyllic site of King Arthur's court.

Only one week after Kennedy was assassinated, Jacqueline Kennedy was interviewed by author Theodore H. White for an article that was to appear in *Life* magazine. In the interview, Jacqueline told White that her husband's favorite song, one that he listened to every evening he could, was from the musical show based on the King Arthur legend. Kennedy's favorite lyric from that production, Jacqueline stated, was, "Don't let it be forgot, that once there was a spot, for one brief shining moment that was known as Camelot."

The *Life* article captured the imagination of the American public. The term "Camelot" came to be used to describe the Kennedy White House years. A book describing Jacqueline's White House restoration was titled *Designing Camelot*. Another, profiling Kennedy's sisters and sisters-in-law, was called *Jackie, Ethel, Joan: The Women of Camelot*. And one describing the elegant way in which Jacqueline Kennedy dressed was titled *Jackie: The Clothes of Camelot*.

As many writers pointed out, it was a natural connection. Like King Arthur and his knights, John Kennedy was movie-star handsome. Like them, he had become a champion of justice. But since the press purposely refrained from writing about a president's private life, there was still no mention of such things as the extramarital affairs Kennedy had had with several women.

The Camelot–Kennedy connection would remain, summed up best by Theodore White in his book *In Search of History*, written almost twenty years after his *Life* article. "The Kennedy administration became Camelot," he wrote, "—a magic moment in American history . . . when great deeds were done, when artists, writers, and poets met at the White House, and the barbarians beyond the walls held back."

ABOVE: Photographs like this one of John and Caroline provided the public with a very personal view of an American presidency.

OPPOSITE: President and Mrs. Kennedy leave the First Anniversary Inaugural Salute dinner. It was images like this, showcasing the glamour and youth of the first couple, that earned them the kind of adulation usually reserved for movie stars and sports heroes.

88

AN ENDURING LEGACY

For a man who was president for so short a time, John Kennedy left behind an enormous legacy. One of his greatest contributions, the Peace Corps, has been operating for more than four decades, has had some two hundred thousand volunteers working in some 140 countries, and is still growing. His physical fitness efforts, particularly those aimed at young people, raised the nation's awareness about this

serious issue, one that is still being addressed today. And while Kennedy did not live to see an American step onto the moon, his vision and determination made it possible.

He bestowed other gifts upon us as well. By negotiating the first nuclear test-ban treaty, he took the first steps toward steering the world away from self-destruction. And he and Jacqueline Kennedy elevated the arts in America to a position they had never before held.

Kennedy, historian Tim Hill wrote, "symbolized the hopes and dreams of a generation." What makes his legacy even stronger is the fact that the words he used to inspire these hopes and dreams are as relevant today as when he spoke them. Perhaps author and historian William Manchester said it best: "[Kennedy's] death was tragic," he wrote, "but his life had been a triumph, and that is how he should be remembered, and celebrated."

ABOVE: High among the many things the world owes to John Kennedy is his vision in reaching for the moon and beyond. Here, Buzz Aldrin, the lunar module pilot of the spacecraft that first took man to the moon, salutes the American flag he and Neil Armstrong placed there.

OPPOSITE: President Bill Clinton, like so many people of his generation, credits John Kennedy with inspiring him to enter public service. As this photograph reveals, a young Clinton actually met Kennedy when the group Boys Nation visited the White House.

PLACES TO VISIT

The following places provide living reminders of John F. Kennedy's life and the times in which he lived. All have special exhibits and programs of interest for young people and are fun to visit.

John F. Kennedy Presidential Library and Museum
Columbia Point
Boston, Massachusetts 02125
For information: 617-514-1600
www.jfklibrary.org

The John F. Kennedy Presidential Library and Museum is dedicated to the memory of the nation's thirty-fifth president. The museum portrays Kennedy's life, leadership, and legacy; conveys his enthusiasm for politics and public service; and illustrates the nature of the office of the president. The many exhibits include those on the space program during his administration, the presidential debates, the First Lady, the 1960 election, Kennedy's speeches at home and abroad, and many others. The museum also houses Kennedy's sailboat *Victura* and a replica of his White House Oval Office.

John Fitzgerald Kennedy National Historic Site
83 Beals Street
Brookline, Massachusetts 02446
For information: 617-566-7937
www.nps.gov/jofi

The John F. Kennedy National Historic Site preserves Kennedy's birthplace. Restored in 1967 by John Kennedy's mother, Rose, each room in the house appears as it did in 1917, when John Kennedy was born. National Park Service guides conduct informative and interesting tours of the house, which is filled with artifacts of John's early years. Items on display include the copious index cards compiled by Rose documenting the ailments and general health of John and his sisters and brothers.

John F. Kennedy Space Center
Kennedy Space Center, Florida 32899
For information: 866-737-5235
www.kennedyspacecenter.com

The Kennedy Space Center Visitor Complex features a host of interesting displays. Included are the Space Launch Experience—a simulation ride into space—and two IMAX theaters featuring three-dimensional films of various aspects of the space exploration experience. There are various bus tours of the large facility, including those to launchpad sites. Transportation is also available to the Apollo/Saturn V Center, which houses a restored Saturn V launch vehicle and an Apollo lunar module, among many other exhibits. Two theaters within the Apollo/Saturn V Center allow the visitor to relive dramatic moments in the Apollo space program.

The Sixth Floor Museum at Dealey Plaza
411 Elm Street
Dallas, Texas 75202
214-747-6660
http://jfk.org

The Sixth Floor Museum at Dealey Plaza is located on the site of the former Texas School Book Depository, which evidence shows is the place from where shots were fired at President Kennedy during his assassination. Former Book Depository employee Lee Harvey Oswald was linked to the shooting and arrested for the president's assassination, which he fervently denied at the time of his own death at the hands of nightclub owner Jack Ruby. Exhibits focus on the assassination and legacy of President John F. Kennedy.

FURTHER READING AND SURFING

Books

Cooper, Ilene. *Jack: The Early Years of John F. Kennedy*. New York: Dutton, 2003.

Hampton, Wilborn. *Kennedy Assassinated! The World Mourns: A Reporter's Story*. Boston: Candlewick, 1997.

Heiligman, Deborah. *High Hopes: A Photobiography of John F. Kennedy*. Washington DC: National Geographic, 2003.

Hodge, Marie. *John F. Kennedy: Voice of Hope*. New York: Sterling, 2007.

Kaplan, Howard S. *John F. Kennedy: A Photographic Story of a Life*. New York: DK Publishing, 2004.

Krull, Kathleen. *The Brothers Kennedy: John, Robert, Edward*. New York: Simon & Schuster, 2010.

Sandler, Martin W. *Presidents*. New York: Harper, 1995.

Sommer, Shelley. *John F. Kennedy: His Life and Legacy*. New York: HarperCollins, 2005.

Stoughton, Cecil, and Chester V. Clifton. *The Memories: JFK 1961–1963*. New York: Norton, 1973.

Time for Kids. *John F. Kennedy: The Making of a Leader*. New York: HarperCollins, 2005.

Web Sites

http://topics.nytimes.com/top/reference/timestopics/people/k/
john_fitzgerald_kennedy/index.html

www.arlingtoncemetery.net/jfk.htm

www.historyplace.com/kennedy

www.jfklibrary.org

www.kennedyspacecenter.com

www.life.com/search/?q0=john+f.+kennedy

www.nps.gov/jofi

www.pbskids.org/wayback/index.html

www.pbs.org/wgbh/americanexperience/films/kennedys

www.whitehouse.gov/about/presidents/johnfkennedy

SOURCES

The following sources have been particularly important in presenting key concepts in this book:

Arthur M. Schlesinger Jr.'s *A Thousand Days: John F. Kennedy in the White House* was written by one of America's most respected historians and is an insightful and intimate portrayal of John F. Kennedy and his administration.

Cecil Stoughton's *The Memories: JFK 1961–1963* is a revealing personal account by one who had unique access to John Kennedy. The book contains scores of photographs taken by Stoughton during the time he served as Kennedy's official White House photographer.

William Manchester's *One Brief Shining Moment: Remembering Kennedy* is arguably the most beautifully written book about John F. Kennedy and contains many revealing quotes from Kennedy and those close to him.

The greatest collection of photographs of Kennedy from his early days through his White House years is housed at the John F. Kennedy Presidential Library and Museum. You can view and study these pictures in the following manner:

- ✦ Go to the Web site www.jfklibrary.org.
- ✦ On the Home page, select Historical Resources, then click on Archives.
- ✦ Next, click on Image Galleries, and then select White House Photographs Gallery.
- ✦ When you have finished viewing these images, go back to Image Galleries and then click on Picture Gallery to view additional pictures.
- ✦ To study more than 3,500 other photographs of John F. Kennedy and subjects relating to him, click on the Begin Search bar on the Archives page mentioned above.
- ✦ Then, in the Search Bar, type: john f kennedy media viewer.

Here is a bibliography of the most significant sources I used in my research:

Adler, Bill. *The Kennedy Wit.* New York: Citadel, 1964.

Dallek, Robert, and Terry Golway. *Let Every Nation Know: John F. Kennedy in His Own Words.* Naperville, Illinois: Sourcebooks, 2006.

Dherbier, Yann-Brice, and Pierre-Henri Verlhac. *John Fitzgerald Kennedy: A Life in Pictures.* New York: Phaidon, 2003.

Faber, Harold. *The Kennedy Years.* New York: Viking, 1964.

Hill, Tim. *JFK & Jackie: Unseen Archives.* New York: Barnes & Noble Books, 2003.

Kennedy, Rose Fitzgerald. *Times to Remember.* New York: Bantam, 1975.

Life in Camelot: The Kennedy Years. Philip Kunhardt Jr., ed. Boston: Little, Brown, 1988.

Lowe, Jacques. *Remembering Jack.* Boston: Bullfinch, 2003.

Manchester, William. *One Brief Shining Moment: Remembering Kennedy.* Boston: Little, Brown, 1983.

Schlesinger, Arthur M., Jr. *A Thousand Days: John. F. Kennedy in the White House.* New York: Black Dog and Leventhal, 2005.

Sorensen, Theodore C. *Kennedy.* New York: Harper & Row, 1965.

Stoughton, Cecil, and Chester V. Clifton. *The Memories: JFK 1961–1963.* New York: Norton, 1973.

KENNEDY QUOTATIONS AND THEIR SOURCES

The quotations that appear within the boxes on each spread are all John F. Kennedy's own words. Below are the sources for these quotations:

Page 4: Inaugural Address, January 20, 1961

Page 6: Address in Frankfurt, Germany, June 25, 1963

Page 8: Address to a Joint Convention of the General Court of the Commonwealth of Massachusetts, January 9, 1961

Page 10: Television address on behalf of the National Cultural Center, November 29, 1962

Page 12: Remarks at the White House to members of the American Legion, March 1, 1962

Page 14: Remarks at a memorial program for the 25th anniversary of the signing of the Social Security Act in Hyde Park, New York, August 14, 1960

Page 16: Commencement Address at American University, June 10, 1963

Page 18: Remarks at the United States Naval Academy, August 1, 1963

Page 20: Message to Roosevelt Day commemoration, January 29, 1961

Page 22: *Profiles in Courage.* New York: Harper, 1956

Page 24: Remarks at Amherst College, October 26, 1963

Page 26: Address at the University of California, Berkeley, March 23, 1962

Page 28: Democratic Party nomination acceptance speech in Los Angeles, California, July 15, 1960

Page 30: Address to the Greater Houston Ministerial Association, September 12, 1960

Page 32: Remark during visit to Paris, May 1961

Page 34: Remark to a crowd in Fort Worth, Texas, November 22, 1963

Page 36: Remarks at Amherst College, October 26, 1963

Page 38: Letter to Monsignor Schieder regarding Catholic Youth Week, 1962

Page 40: Address at the University of California, Berkeley, March 23, 1962

Page 42: Address to the National Press Club in Washington DC, January 14, 1960

Page 44: UNICEF appeal, July 25, 1963

Page 46: Remarks to student participants in the White House Seminar in Government, August 27, 1963

Page 48: Address before the 18th General Assembly of the United Nations, September 20, 1963

Page 50: Special Message to the Congress on Urgent National Needs, May 25, 1961

Page 52: "The Soft American." *Sports Illustrated*, December 26, 1960

Page 54: Remarks upon signing the Maternal and Child Health and Mental Retardation Planning Bill, October 24, 1963

Page 56: Quoted in *"Johnny, We Hardly Knew Ye"* by Kenneth P. O'Donnell and David F. Powers; New York: Pocket Books, 1973

Page 58: Press conference, April 21, 1961

Page 60: Radio and television report on the Berlin crisis, July 25, 1961

Page 62: Remarks in the Rudolph Wilde Platz, West Berlin, Germany, June 26, 1963

Page 64: Address before the Irish Parliament, June 28, 1963

Page 66: Address before the 16th General Assembly of the United Nations, September 25, 1961

Page 68: Quoted in *The Remarkable Kennedys* by Joe McCarthy; New York: Popular Library, 1960

Page 70: Radio and television report on Civil Rights, June 11, 1963

Page 72: Radio and television report on Civil Rights, June 11, 1963

Page 74: Remarks at the America Cup dinner in Newport, Rhode Island, September 14, 1962

Page 76: Quoted in *The Mortal Presidency: Illness and Anguish in the White House* by Robert E. Gilbert; New York: Fordham University Press, 1998

Page 78: Remarks to the State and National Democratic Committees in New York, October 12, 1960

Page 80: Remarks at Amherst College, October 26, 1963

INDEX

This book is dedicated to Elizabeth Hodgkin, whose courage, wit, and intelligence inspires us all

First published in the United States of America in January 2011 by Walker Publishing Company, Inc., a division of Bloomsbury Publishing, Inc.
www.bloomsburykids.com

For information about permission to reproduce selections from this book, write to Permissions, Walker BFYR, 175 Fifth Avenue, New York, New York 10010

Library of Congress Cataloging-in-Publication Data
Sandler, Martin W.
Kennedy through the lens : how photography and television revealed and shaped an extraordinary leader / Martin W. Sandler.
p.   cm.
ISBN 978-0-8027-2160-0 (hardcover) • ISBN 978-0-8027-2161-7 (reinforced)
1. Kennedy, John F. (John Fitzgerald), 1917–1963—Pictorial works—Juvenile literature. 2. Kennedy, John F. (John Fitzgerald), 1917–1963—Influence—Juvenile literature.
3. Presidents—United States—Pictorial works—Juvenile literature. 4. Photography—United States—History—20th century—Juvenile literature. I. Title.
E842.Z9S27 2011   973.922092—dc22   2010011103

Book design by Patrick Collins
Typeset in Sabon
Printed in China by C&C Offset Printing Co., Ltd., Shenzhen, Guangdong
1 3 5 7 9 10 8 6 4 2 (hardcover)
1 3 5 7 9 10 8 6 4 2 (reinforced)

All papers used by Bloomsbury Publishing, Inc., are natural, recyclable products made from wood grown in well-managed forests.
The manufacturing processes conform to the environmental regulations of the country of origin.

Acknowledgments

I am indebted to Sam Rubin and Laurie Austin of the John F. Kennedy Presidential Library and Museum for their most appreciated help and suggestions. I am grateful also for the continual assistance I received from Mary Kate Castellani. A debt of gratitude is owed also to Katherine Worten for her many contributions and to Donna Mark and Patrick Collins for the beautiful design they brought to this book. Again, I want to thank Chandra Wohleber, Jennifer Healey, and Melissa Kavonic for so thoroughly checking the accuracy of every statement. And, as always, Carol Sandler's research skills and encouragement have been invaluable. Finally, I have once again been blessed with having Emily Easton to guide me and to help shape this book. Emily, you are the best, and I am most grateful.

Picture Credits

Front cover photograph by Robert Knudsen/John F. Kennedy Presidential Library and Museum; spine and back cover photographs by Cecil Stoughton/John F. Kennedy Presidential Library and Museum.

Courtesy of Corbis Images: page 91; *courtesy of Getty Images:* page 69; *courtesy of Granger Collection:* page 27; *courtesy of John F. Kennedy Foundation:* page 68; *courtesy of John F. Kennedy Presidential Library and Museum:* front endpapers, pages 1, 3, 5, 7, 8, 9, 11, 12, 13, 14, 15, 16, 17, 19, 20, 21, 22, 24, 25, 28, 29, 31, 32, 33, 34, 36, 37, 38, 39, 42, 44, 45, 46, 47, 48–49, 51, 52, 53, 54, 56, 57, 60, 61, 63, 64, 65, 67, 70, 74, 75, 79, 85, 88, 89, 92, back endpaper; *courtesy of Library of Congress:* pages 6, 10, 23, 26, 35, 41, 58, 66, 72, 73, 76, 77, 82, 84, 86, 87, 93; *courtesy of NASA:* page 50; *courtesy of estate of Thurman Naylor:* pages 59, 93; *courtesy of Ronald W. Reagan Presidential Library:* page 40; *courtesy of Wikimedia Commons:* pages 4, 18, 30, 43, 55 (top), 55 (bottom), 62, 71, 78, 80, 81, 83, 90*

"We in this country, in this generation, are—by destiny rather than choice—the watchmen on the walls of world freedom. We ask, therefore, that we may be worthy of our power and responsibility, that we may exercise our strength with wisdom and restraint, and that we may achieve in our time and for all time the ancient vision of 'peace on earth, good will toward men.' That must always be our goal, and the righteousness of our cause must always underlie our strength."

—JOHN F. KENNEDY,
from the speech he was about to deliver
when he was assassinated